A JOURNEY OF SELF DISCOVERY
101 key questions to self exploration

David Routt

Copyright © September 2018

CONTENTS

Chapter one 1

Introduction 1

Chapter two 11

The pilgrimage to self-discovery 11

Chapter three 15

The reliable approach and steps to self-discovery.....15

Chapter four 23

The 11 universal laws (the unique inescapable
universal order)...23

Chapter five...38

101 self-discovery questions......................................38

Chapter six..55

Conclusion 55

CHAPTER ONE

INTRODUCTION

Life is full of "noise." By noise, I mean distractions and all manner of disturbances that surrounds our environment. As humans, we all must have in one way or the other been distracted or influenced by family, peer groups, culture or tradition. We tend to respond or conform to these distractions and act in accordance with the social pressure and lose focus on who we truly are.

"To be yourself in a world that is constantly trying to make you something else is the greatest achievement."

– Ralph Waldo Emerson

The fact is that, if you don't make a conscious attempt and effort to realize the unconscious, which lies deep within you, you will be stereotyped to some belief systems, general pattern or idea of doing things, which hinders the awareness of self.

The essence of this piece of art is to enable you to:

- Disengage from past occurrences or events.

- Be open-minded to understand the structure that regulates your life.

- Discover who you are indeed, and to achieve maximum satisfaction and accomplishment in all areas of life, using well-structured questions on self-discovery.

As Socrates once said, "An unexamined life is not worth living," self-examination is a basic tool for achieving self-awareness, which leads to self-actualization. You can only live a fulfilled life when you live according to your passion and values. Once your ambition, anxiety, and purpose are clearly understood, you'll become much more self-secured and confident. Most importantly, when you're able to accept your weaknesses rather than just focus on your strengths, you'll become more self-aware. Deep within every human lies a creative power and cravings to make a difference in life, to add value to the environment she lives in."

Some school of thought would say, keep living as long as you can and do whatever you can. Eventually, you will discover yourself. That is wholly inactive, and I would rather call it a utopia which is impossible to achieve. You must consciously examine yourself to quicken your self-awareness.

It's in knowing who you truly are that you can make choices or take decisions that are more authentic and reliable. Is your take on a particular issue based on your past, previous mistakes or failures? Your lack of self-discovery can influence your sense of value or definition, your attitude towards failure, your capacity to set personal goals and still leave you in the past.

It's a routine for us as humans to assume that we know ourselves but we end up finding out that all we know is our body or skin color. One of the exciting parts of self-discovery is the journey of knowing yourself beyond your physical body and existing suppositions. A good number of people that have not considered a trip to self-discovery live with the beliefs, opinions of families and groups they belong.

This book offers the right approach to self-awareness, and it seeks to open the minds of people from all areas of life to the reality of nature and the universe at large. It is a conscious effort to ensure that people can identify and appreciate what lies within them and also know who they are indeed.

CHAPTER TWO
THE PILGRIMAGE TO SELF-DISCOVERY

With all manner of certainty, I can assure you that the moment you embark on the lane of self-discovery, turning back on it will be your last option. The fantastic thing about this journey is the effect it carries which include; direction, clarity of purpose and satisfaction which makes it a ride worth embarking.

Basically, "Life will have no meaning if we do not consciously make meaning out of it, and purpose is the only driving force that can lead us to the path that makes life meaningful." It is only when you discover yourself that you can find a purpose which leads to self-actualization.

There was a time I got involved with doing what I didn't really like, but I kept doing it. Some of my peers loved playing football because they had a passion for it but I never enjoyed the game because of the phobia I had for injuries. Most times, I would get back home with the same injury I dreaded most. I wasn't truthful with myself, but somehow I quit playing the game. I'm not implying that you cannot develop your skills in whatever you are doing over a period but my opinion here is that you should instead develop yourself on the things you are passionate about. It has to be something you do and not bother about the time spent in doing them and the risks involved.

The journey will reveal what your beliefs are and it will also enable you to either live by or change them. It may entail you cutting off some people from your life who pose as set back or negative influence, forsaking some negative habits and setting high but realistic goals.

However, the discovery of oneself comes with numerous benefits but to mention a few:

- Increased intelligence: The ability to learn and purposely apply knowledge effectively.

- Increased self-awareness which will enable you to be more consistent.

- Increased ability to free you from the stress of sadness and sickness, which leads to sound health and general well-being.

- The huge capacity to succeed in any chosen career.

- Increased capacity to become self-aware; leading to making more deliberate decisions.

- A positive shift in the capacity and skills to control your mind and emotions.

CHAPTER THREE

THE RELIABLE APPROACH AND STEPS TO SELF-DISCOVERY

- **Approach**

In the quest for self-discovery, it is imperative to take cognizance of things, and then you'll realize why they occur, the reason for your behavior and how you feel.

Nonetheless, the peregrination is challenging because it entails a rigorous examination of your life decisions. You need to keep your mind open and be ready to make some rugged choices and not break them on the short run, but you may have to modify them on the long term.

Often, I liken the approach to self-discovery to a proper diagnosis from a good and trusted medical laboratory towards the appropriate prescription and treatment of any ailment. It saves time, and it's cost effective when we choose the right approach to accomplishing a task. No wonder Arnold Glasow said, "Success isn't complex when you do what is right, in the right way and at the right time."

It is also good to note that your goals might have a shift in the long run as you get to discover yourself and it shouldn't scare you. This is very normal in the journey. You must demonstrate curiosity and a clear mind to have your view without prejudice.

- **Steps**

Step 1: Be honest with yourself

In answering the self-discovery question, you need to be honest and real to yourself. There's no need being dishonest. Self-acceptance will give you the opportunity to discover the truth about yourself and will not allow you to live with the existing condition.

> *"Honesty is the safest way to avoid a mistake from turning into a failure."*
>
> –James Altucher

Step 2: Be ready for a change

You will be exceedingly grateful for whatever you discover about yourself. However, have it in mind that "Change is constant," and you need to embrace it consciously.

> *"The changes you see around you are as a result of the changes that happen within you."*
>
> –Victor E.

Step 3: Beyond the physical

Self-discovery would be futile without seeking to know your actual purpose here on earth from the Creator of the universe. You need to be open-minded, honest and ready for change and then seek the Creator's purpose for your life.

"Just as a candle cannot burn without fire, men cannot live without a spiritual life."
–Buddha

Step 4: Keep the right company

In the quest for self-discovery, you need the right company that encourages your growth. If you surround yourself with the wrong people, then you will be no better than the old and unreal version of yourself.

"A good company in a journey makes it appear shorter."
–Izak Walton

Step 5: Establish your core values

Your core values define your personality and determine every move you make towards self-discovery. It also helps you figure out if you are in the right direction and complying with your purpose by creating a steady guide.

Below are some types of core values:

- Positivity

- Reliability

- Efficiency

- Consistency

- Open-mindedness

- Passion

- Innovation

- Commitment

- Perseverance

- Motivation.

"A core value is only valid when you live by it."

–Victor E.

Step 6: Create a perfect picture of your future self

Picture yourself in a condition of absolute self-actualization, in perfect old age and ask yourself the following questions:

- What are the things I would have done better if I were to be younger?

- What are the things I would have learned, that will yield the best possible outcome or effect in my life? Ensure that your answers are given the necessary action.

"To carry a positive action, we must develop here a positive vision."

–Dalai Lama

CHAPTER FOUR

THE 11 UNIVERSAL LAWS (THE UNIQUE INESCAPABLE UNIVERSAL ORDER)

Discussed here are indeed inescapable laws, also known as "The Universal Laws." You can't escape from them as they apply to you directly or indirectly. Thus, it's better for you to consider these laws directly and see how you can profit from them instead of allowing them to take effect in your life indirectly.

Why I use the word "inescapable" is not farfetched; it comes from the fact that your ignorance of these laws cannot exempt you from its establishment. The law is constant for everyone as long as you are a part of the universe.

The fusion of these laws in this material cannot be over-emphasized as it will significantly open your mind to the effectiveness of the journey. The knowledge, understanding, and application of these systems will also guarantee your inner peace and fulfillment.

[1]   The Law of Divine Oneness

The law of divine oneness states that everything is connected to everything else. Whatever we think, believe, say or do will have a corresponding effect on others and the universe around us regardless of the distance or proximity of the people.

This law makes us understand that for us to have lasting happiness and fulfillment in life; we must love unconditionally and contribute to others through our passion in spite of what those passions are. It may be cooking, tailoring, teaching spirituality, etc.

[2]   The Law of Vibration and Attraction

The law of vibration states that everything in the universe vibrates and travels in a circular pattern. Our thoughts, desires, feelings and sound forms a certain vibration and they are sent out to the universe. People or things that match our vibration frequency get attracted into our life, be it our desire or fears. In other words, the people or object that comes to us is as a result of the vibration we send to the universe. The rich will also get richer because they focus on wealth and it comes to them while the poor get poorer because of their negative thoughts.

[3] The Law of Perpetual Transmutation of Energy

Understanding the universal laws will enable you to know that the power to change your life energies or situation lies within you. The picture we create in our mind continuously will transform into reality in our life. Superior vibrations consume and convert lower ones. Therefore, we must get rid of every negative thought and conceive only positive thoughts in every situation to achieve fulfillment in life.

[4]   The Law of Cause and Effect

Everything that happens in our life revolves around the universal laws. All our dreams, thoughts and actions have reactions or repercussions. We basically reap what we sow, be it in our thoughts, words, and actions.

I remember a young woman in my early 20s who kept declaring that even in her next generation, she will never need a husband and she could always make babies out of wedlock if she wishes. Years later, I met her at the Galleria - Houston, Texas, when I went shopping with my wife, and kid and we exchanged pleasantries. I asked after her family, and she took a deep breath and exhaled. I could see the disappointment on her face, then she said, she was still single. At that point, I remembered what she said in the past. She went on telling me that she admires my family and she wishes to be like me.

I left her with these words: "The results you get in your life now are the aftermath of your decisions in the past." If you desire a new and positive effect in your tomorrow, you'll have to start now to decide on a positive and new cause of action.

[5]   The Law of Action

The law of action must be applied in order for our thoughts and dreams to be made evident on earth. In other words, as co-creators in the universe, our actions should be geared towards the actualization of our thoughts, dreams, and words.

A story was once told of two friends who visited a seer to know what their future holds. The soothsayer looked at one of them and said, "Long live the king" and immediately he heard those words, he left the place and started jubilating in celebration as a future king, even when he didn't look like one. The seer turned to the other person and said, "You will die in poverty." He was sober, but he resolved in his heart to be successful. Consequently, he started farming to avert the prophecy given to him by the soothsayer. Years later, he became very successful, possessing goods in abundance with male and female servants.

There was an extreme shortage of food where his friend was living, still daydreaming and waiting for his kingdom to manifest. In their search for food, the residents of his town found the diligent man and his supplies in abundance. They begged him to become their king, agreeing to serve him in exchange for food to survive the famine. That was how a man who was degraded and 'sentenced' to death became king while the anticipated king remained poor all his life.

The story confirms the law of action in play. Direct actions must be taken for your dreams, thoughts, and words to manifest on earth.

"You cannot dream yourself into character; you must hammer and forge yourself one."

\- James A. Froude

[6]   The Law of Gender

This law states that everything in nature is masculine and feminine; they are both required for life to exist. The law is seen in the animal kingdom as sex, and it governs creation.

Furthermore, before anything reaches maturity, it must undergo a period of gravidity and growth, and it's our duty to harmonize the masculine and feminine forces within us to become joint creators with the universal awareness.

As humans, our thoughts are also governed by the same law and must pass through the same stages of gestation and development, before they become a reality. We need to be determined, patient and then believe for our purposes to show up or manifest.

[7]   The Law of Relativity

We are bound to face problems or challenges in life. This law teaches us to compare our problems to other issues in its opposite view. No matter how bad we view our situation to be, there's always someone in a worst condition. This law gives hope to anyone having a challenge in any area of life, to understand that there's always someone out there facing a worst case. It also gives us reasons to cheer up, no matter the situation you find yourself.

[8]   The Law of Rhythm

Everything dances to certain rhythms. Seasons, stages, cycles and patterns, are established by these rhythms. Each cycle shows the consistency of God's creation. Sunset after sunrise, night comes after day. After spring comes, summer and autumn come after summer and winter follow, and the cycle starts all over and over again till infinity.

When it seems like things are going down, don't feel awful or terrible for change will come and things will get better and the good times will show up.

[9]   The Law of Polarity

This law states that in every bad, there is good, everything has an opposite, Top-Bottom, Good-Bad, Hot-Cold, Weak-Strong. Learn to focus on the good when faced with challenges instead of looking at the adverse effect of the troubles. Always see the light at the end of the trouble.

[10] The Law of Correspondence

The law of correspondence states that the laws of physics that expound the physical world energy, light, vibration, and motion have their relationship with the universal principles. "As above so below."

To break this down, you are bound to fail if your beliefs and attitude don't match or tally with your purpose. The law of correspondence and the law of attraction will fail if your attitudes and beliefs are contrary to your purpose.

[11]   The Law of Compensation

The law of compensation dishes out to us the laws of cause and effect and action in the form of blessings and riches made available to us. The corresponding result of our actions rewards us in the form of money, gifts, friendship, property or blessings.

In other words, the universe will always reward our actions with those things that make life beautiful and more enjoyable.

The understanding, meditation, and application of these universal laws will guarantee your inner peace, as it has given me

the required fulfillment in life.

CHAPTER FIVE

101 SELF-DISCOVERY QUESTIONS

Before I list out the questions, it is important to note that your initial answers to these questions are not very significant. Your failure to give the right answer is inevitable and quite normal. In other words, don't stress about getting it correctly. All that is required is an answer.

What is more important is the application of this information to improve the quality of your life to achieve self-actualization. You do that by reasoning. You will discover things that are harmful and things that are of immense benefit to yourself.

Try as much as you can to destroy things that are harmful to you and give preference to things of benefit.

You can achieve that by:

- Staying away from things you are not good at; focus more on the things that give you joy.

- Doing more things you are good at; invest your time on the things you are passionate about.

- Avoiding things that make you sad.

It is also imperative to note that every individual has a distinctive view and answers to the questions.

Furthermore, these prompts will give you direction, leading to self-actualization, accomplishment, and fulfillment as it will cover virtually every aspect of life including business and profession, leisure, prosperity and wellbeing, feelings and emotion, family and acquaintance as well as the supernatural.

Finally, find below the questions leading to self-discovery and actualization.

1.   What's my purpose here on earth?

This is a major question that hits on the basics of your mission in life. Without purpose, you can't accomplish life's mission. As humans, we are here for a purpose, and each of our talents, strength, and activities should be driven towards accomplishing our mission.

2.   What's my major fear?

Fear is one thing that can prevent you from living your best, and on the contrary, it can also stimulate or motivate you to be innovative and work tirelessly to archiving success. You can only begin to alleviate the risk presented by your fears when you identify it. You'll be brave when you take the decision and find out that your fears are merely perception, they do not exist. What doesn't kill you makes you stronger.

3. Five things I would have accomplished if weren't so scared.

4. What gives me happiness?

I'm sure there are two or more things that make you happy and joyful. Outline those things that make you glad indeed. It may be the simplest things that put a smile on your face. If you haven't found anything that makes you happy, then you should deliberately make your life joyful.

"According to Maria Montessori, personal health is related to self-control and the worship of life in all its natural beauty-self-control bringing with it happiness, renewed youth, and long life."

5. 10-15 words that describe me.

6. What am I optimistic about and why? What are those things I'm so positive and confident about and see only the bright side of it?

7. What am I pessimistic about and why? What are those things I have negative feelings about?

8. What part of the body am I most thankful for and why?

9. My thoughts on the first impression people have of me. Do I think people have a good or bad first impression about me?

10. What do I like about myself? The things you like about yourself could be a major factor or quality to help boost your self-esteem and make you stand out in your chosen career.

11. What are the things I want to change about myself? It could be some habits or thoughts.

12. Have I discovered my talents? Talent can be seen as a natural ability someone has without being taught.

13. Have I activated my talents and how? It is only when you activate a SIM card that you can start using it.

14. How best can I utilize my talents?

15. What skills would I like to acquire? A list of things you need to learn and ensure that you learn them. Be willing to move away from your comfort zone. You will gain more knowledge and experience.

16. Do I belong in the past, present or future moments and why?

17. What are the things that make or spoil my day? The events that ruin or make my day meaningful.

18. Do I easily get worried? How do I deal with it?

19. What makes me happy?

20. Have I ever done something terrible out of anger? Something I feel awful about, after my action. What was the act?

21. What's my definition of success? My description of success.

22. Am I scared of success?

23. What are the things I keep doing that restricts my success?

24. Do I find myself successful and why?

25. What makes me beat my chest and say; "I'm proud of myself?"

26. Who are my role models? Do they have good qualities to inspire me? A model is one who is worthy of being exemplary for your business or any chosen career of your life.

27. Do I delay or even give up easily? Do I get things done on time?

28. What are my childhood experiences? What have I learned from them?

29. What are my adulthood experiences? What have I learned from them?

30. What were my future ambitions as a child?

31. How would I live a day free of consequences?

32. What are the things I wish others knew about me?

33. Am I dependable? Reasons for my answer.

34. Am I open-minded or not? Reasons for my answer.

35. What is the best advice I have ever received?

36. Do I really believe in my instinct and why?

37. Do I follow the crowd or do I speak up? What energizes or motivates me?

38. What are my regrets? How can I live above them?

39. What is always responsible for my tears?

40. Can I boldly say I'm a good friend? Reasons for my answer.

41. Do I have a best friend?

42. How would my friend describe me?

43. Outline the qualities a friend should possess.

44. Who is my oldest friend and what do I like most about this person?

45. That little thing I enjoy with a special person in my life.

46. What do I enjoy best about being single?

47. What do I enjoy most about being married?

48. A brief description of a difficult person in my life.

49. Do I forgive easily or not?

50. What do I think about unconditional love?

51. Do I care about what people think about me? Reasons for my answer.

52. A list of people I trust in my life, which genuinely supports me.

53. A ruthful way I've been supportive to a friend lately. How can I replicate it to myself?

54. What are the things I am doing now that I wish I did five years ago?

55. What's my projection for ten years from now?

56. What is the state of my physical health? In what ways am I healthy or not?

57. Am I mentally healthy? Reasons for my answers.

58. What is the state of my emotional health? How am I healthy or not?

59. Have I recently cared for my mental health and how?

60. Have I recently cared for my physical health and how?

61. Have I recently cared for my emotional health and how?

62. How do I appreciate my wellness whenever I'm sick?

63. What's my take on spirituality?

64. What do I believe about God?

65. Have I ever felt most attached to my spiritual side and how?

66. What's my take on wisdom? What's my source of wisdom in life?

67. What are the principles that guide my spiritual life?

68. Am I spiritually healthy? What are the reasons for your answer?

69. Do I believe in things happening by chance? Reasons for my answer.

70. Do I believe I have a soul? Believing that there's life beyond the physical body, (Life after Death). Reasons for my answer.

71. The persons or figures that have greatly impacted on my spirituality?

72. What spiritual theory or practice do I find most significant? The activities that best connect me to my creator.

73. What do I believe is enough for me and why?

74. The liberty or freedom I'm most grateful for and why?

75. A list of things I want to say yes to.

76. A list of things I want to say no to.

77. What has been my greatest surprise in life? My most shocking experience.

78. Which moment do I consider the most fun moment of my life?

79. Assuming there's a natural disaster and I'm to leave my home, what are the four most important things I will take along with me?

80. Am I a giver or a taker? Reason for my answer.

81. What I enjoy most about my job.

82. The major lessons I've learnt from my current or previous job.

83. Is my current career path in harmony with who I am and what I want to be, or is it time to follow the right path?

84. Ten things I take for granted, that may be lacking in other parts of the world.

85. When it comes to money, what's my belief?

86. If I'm to write a short letter to money, describing the kind of relationship I would like to have with them as fellow humans, what would the content be?

87. If I'm given 20 million dollars in cash and I'm limited to just 48 hours to spend it, how would I spend it? I have to analyze my spending critically, even to the last unit.

88. What are my top three short-term goals and objectives?

89. What are my top three strategic or long-term plans?

90. Things I've done lately that I thought I could never do.

91. What do I do with my free time?

92. What are my favorite books and why I love them?

93. My preferred or favorite movies and why I love them?

94. What are my favorite songs and why I love them?

95. What is my best part of nature?

96. How best do I enjoy nature?

97. How was my last holiday spent?

98. My best season and what makes it special to me?

99. Which day do I consider as my best in the week and why?

100. Which week do I consider as my best in the month and why?

101. Which month do I consider as my best in the year and why?

102. Which day do I consider as my worst in the week and why?

103. Which week do I consider as my worst in the month and why?

104. Which month do I consider as my worst in the year and why?

105. What are the major things I like about my country?

106. What can I invent or add to my environment to make life better?

107. Do I think before speaking or acting?

CHAPTER SIX

CONCLUSION

Self-discovery is an endless journey that makes you aware of your inner self. I classify it to be a journey of a lifetime. What lies within us is not permanent but dynamic in the sense that, changes are bound to occur at any point we get to discover ourselves, and those changes are consciously made by us.

This journal is to serve as a prerequisite to making better decisions in every area of life. It will to a large extent, enhance the clarity of purpose and action sent to the universe. The universe, in turn, responds to every action sent, be it positive or negative, therefore confirming the law of cause and action without any form of obstacle or hindrance. You'll also attract the people or things that vibrate in line with your being.

Spirituality is a significant factor you can't rule out from any discovery. Your purpose must be in harmony with the purpose of the creator of the universe, and you must seek his divine purpose for your life. No one is a mishap. There's a unique purpose for every individual here on earth and your ability to discover your divine purpose gives you fulfillment and all round satisfaction in life.